CW01360266

WORLD COMMUNITY

By Steffi Cavell-Clarke

Our Values

©This edition was published in 2018.
First published in 2017.

Book Life
King's Lynn
Norfolk PE30 4LS

ISBN: 978-1-78637-115-7

All rights reserved
Printed in Malaysia

Written by:
Steffi Cavell-Clarke

Edited by:
Grace Jones

Designed by:
Natalie Carr

A catalogue record for this book is available from the British Library.

CONTENTS

PAGE 4 — What Are Our Values?
PAGE 6 — Our Community
PAGE 8 — Why Is It Important?
PAGE 10 — Different Cultures
PAGE 12 — Cultures in Our Community
PAGE 14 — People Who Help Us
PAGE 16 — Listening to Others
PAGE 18 — Our Community at School
PAGE 20 — Our Community at Home
PAGE 22 — Making a Difference
PAGE 24 — Glossary and Index

Words that look like **this** can be found in the glossary on page 24.

WHAT ARE OUR VALUES?

Values are ideas and beliefs that help us to work and live together in a **community**. Values teach us how to behave and how we should **respect** each other and ourselves.

Our Values

- Respecting Others
- Making Your Own Choices
- Understanding Different Faiths
- Being Responsible
- Helping Others
- Respecting the Law
- Sharing Your Ideas
- Listening to Others

5

OUR COMMUNITY

A community is a group of people that might live in the same area, or share similar attitudes and values. A person can be part of one, a few or many different communities.

Different types of community can be found all around the world. Each and every community is important whether it is a large city community or a small village community.

Tulear, Madagascar

Tokyo, Japan

WHY IS IT IMPORTANT?

Living in a community allows us to make friends and work together to solve problems. Communities can also give us a sense of **belonging** and acceptance.

It is important that we care for other people in our community and help to try and keep each other safe.

Everyone in the world is part of one big community, so we should be kind and caring towards everybody.

DIFFERENT CULTURES

Cultures are the ideas and behaviours of groups of people. Each community has its own culture, but it can also welcome new and different cultures.

Different cultures may have particular **traditions** or hold special celebrations throughout the year. People in many different communities celebrate Chinese New Year. People can celebrate the festival in many ways, such as wearing traditional clothing or taking part in large street parades.

CULTURES IN OUR COMMUNITY

A community can have many people with different cultures. It can also include people of different religions and **nationalities**. This is called a **multicultural** community.

It is important that we always welcome people into our communities and accept their cultures, beliefs and traditions, even if they are different from our own.

PEOPLE WHO HELP US

There are people in our communities who have special jobs. They help to keep us safe, and help the community in different ways.

Police officers, doctors, and firefighters are able to help us in an **emergency**. It is important that we respect them and don't get in their way when they are trying to do their jobs.

LISTENING TO OTHERS

We all have the **freedom** to express our cultures in our communities, and it is important that we accept others too. We can do this by listening to others and trying to understand their culture.

Jessica goes to church every Sunday with her family. They meet other members of the community there. They sing and pray to God together.

MAKING A DIFFERENCE

It can be difficult for someone to settle into a new community, so it is important that we welcome them and make them feel at home. We can do this by saying hello and being friendly.

Remember to always tell your parent or the person who looks after you before speaking to a stranger.

We can help our community by helping the **environment**. We can do this by throwing our litter in a rubbish bin and reusing plastic shopping bags.

GLOSSARY

belonging	being part of something
emergency	a dangerous problem that requires action
environment	your surroundings
freedom	being allowed to do something
law	rules that a community has to follow
multicultural	different cultures in a community
nationalities	people who come from the same nation or country
respect	feeling that something or someone is important
responsible	to be trusted to do the right thing
traditions	ways of behaving that have been done over a long time

INDEX

beliefs 4, 13
cultures 10–13, 16, 20
families 17, 20–21
friends 8, 19, 22
homes 20–22
jobs 14-15
listening 5, 16–18
religions 12
respect 4–5, 15, 18
schools 18–19
traditions 11, 13, 20
values 4–6, 20

PHOTO CREDITS

Photocredits: Abbreviations: l–left, r –right, b –bottom, t –top, c-centre, m –middle.
Front Cover – 2 - 3 - Raw pixel.com. 4 - Rawpixel.com. 5tl - Monkey Business Images. 5tm - Tom Wang. 5tr - Yuliya Evstratenko. 5ml - Andresr. 5mr - ISchmidt. 5bl - Lucian Milasan. 5bm - Pressmaster. 5br - Luis Molinero.. 6 - Pressmaster.7t - sunsinger. 7b - Matej Kastelic. 8 - pio3. 9 - MNStudio. 10 - Zurijeta. 11 - Sergei Bachlakov. 12 - Monkey Business Images. 13 - Monkey Business Images. 14 - Pressmaster. 15 - SanchaiRat. 16 - CristinaMuraca. 17 - Migel. 18 - stefanolunardi. 19 - szefei. 20 - Denis Kuvaev. 21 - Blend Images. 22 - Pressmaster. 23 - wavebreakmedia.
Images are courtesy of Shutterstock.com. With thanks to Getty Images, Thinkstock Photo and iStockphoto.